BY VALERIE BODDEN

Published in 2011 by Franklin Watts
338 Euston Road
London NW1 3BH

Franklin Watts Australia
Level 17/207 Kent Street
Sydney NSW 2000

First published by Creative Education
P.O. Box 227, Mankato, Minnesota 56002
Creative Education is an imprint of The Creative Company
www.thecreativecompany.us

ISBN 978 1 4451 0589 5
Dewey number: 918.1'1

Design and production by The Design Lab
Art direction by Rita Marshall
Printed in the United States of America

Photographs by 123RF (Dmitry Rukhlenko), Big Stock Photo
(Bobby Singapore), Corbis (Corbis Sygma, Wolfgang Kaehler, Layne
Kennedy, Danny Lehman, Buddy Mays, Reuters, Galen Rowell,
Kevin Schafer, Sea World of California, Nik Wheeler, Staffan
Widstrand), Dreamstime (Sunheyy), iStockphoto (Emre Ogan)

Every attempt has been made to clear copyright. Should there be any
inadvertent omission, please contact the publisher for rectification.

Franklin Watts is a division of Hachette Children's Books,
an Hachette UK company.
www.hachette.co.uk

Printed in China

# RIVER AMAZON

**W**

FRANKLIN WATTS
LONDON • SYDNEY

River Amazon

SOUTH AMERICA

The Amazon is the second longest river in the world, after the River Nile. It is found in the **continent** of South America. The River Amazon flows through the countries of Peru, Colombia and Brazil. It ends in the Atlantic Ocean.

The Amazon River takes many twists and turns on its journey through South America to the sea. Big bends in a river are called meanders.

People sometimes call the Amazon the 'Ocean River' because ships can travel far down it.

The River Amazon is about 6,400 km long and, at its widest, around 50 kilometres wide. It holds more water than any other river in the world.

The Amazon is the biggest **river basin** in the world (left), covering over seven million square kilometres.

Scientists think that the River Amazon used to flow west towards the Pacific Ocean millions of years ago. But then the mighty Andes Mountains formed. They blocked the river's path. So it began to flow east towards the Atlantic Ocean instead.

When the river has to flow over tall rocks, it creates a waterfall (right). The water wears away the rock, making the waterfall bigger and moving it gradually backwards.

A waterfall in the Amazon Basin, Venezuela.

Many people live near the Amazon in both small villages and big cities.

The weather around the River Amazon is warm all year round and there is a lot of rainfall. The Amazon **floods** every year, so homes nearby are often built on **stilts** to stay dry.

The city of Belém (left) on the banks of the Amazon in Brazil is a busy port.

Much of the land around the River Amazon is covered by **rainforest**. Many rare and wonderful animals are **native** to the rainforest. Monkeys, jaguars and iguanas live in the rainforest. So do parrots and sloths.

Iguanas (above) and parrots (opposite) are rainforest animals.

About half of all the kinds of birds in the world live near the River Amazon.

The Amazon's pirarucu (*pih-RAH-rih-koo*) is one of the world's biggest freshwater fish.

Fish such as deadly piranhas (*pih-RAH-nuhs*) swim in the River Amazon. So do **mammals** such as pink river dolphins and **manatees**. Snakes live in the water, too. Giant Amazon water lilies float on the river's surface.

About 20 kinds of piranhas (above) live in the River Amazon.

Native peoples have lived near the River Amazon for thousands of years. Over time, they have learned to live alongside the river and the rainforest. Their food, clothes and medicines all come from the Amazon and the rainforest.

Many native people travel on the river in wooden canoes.

Over the years, people have cut down many trees near the Amazon for wood. They have **polluted** the water. They have built **dams** on the rivers that join the Amazon. This has damaged the river, but today, many people work to protect it.

Large rainforest trees are cut down and made into wooden boards for houses.

Many people visit the Amazon every year. They take boat rides down the river. They fish in the water. And they are amazed by all the plants and animals in the Amazon rainforest!

Some visitors take a trip down the Amazon on cruise ships.

CLIPPER ADVENTURER

Plants and fruits from the Amazon rainforest, such as cocoa beans, are used to make medicines.

# Glossary

**continent** one of Earth's seven big pieces of land

**dams** walls built across rivers to hold water back

**floods** when water overflows onto land that is normally dry

**mammals** animals that suckle their young

**manatees** big water animals with paddle-shaped front flippers

**native** original; native peoples were the first to live in an area

**polluted** made dirty with chemicals or other things

**rainforest** thick forest where there is a lot of rainfall

**river basin** the area of land that is drained by a river and all the smaller rivers that lead into it

**stilts** tall posts that hold a building off the ground

# Read More about It

*Espresso Ideas Box: Rainforests* by Deborah Chancellor (Franklin Watts, 2011)

*Saving Wildlife: Rainforest Animals* by Sonya Newland (Franklin Watts, 2010)

*Voices of the Rainforest* by Mick Manning and Brita Granström (Franklin Watts, 2007)

# Index